Also available in this series from Quadrille:

MINDFULNESS
QUIET
FRIENDSHIP
LOVE
CONFIDENCE
TIDINESS
HAPPINESS
MOTHERHOOD
LUCK
US
SEX
CHRISTMAS
SISTERHOOD
SELF-CARE
KINDNESS
BRIDESMAIDS
PRIDE
GRATITUDE
POSITIVITY
UNITY
HOPE
JOY
COURAGE
MANIFESTING
SELF-LOVE

the little book of
RESILIENCE

Hardie Grant

QUADRILLE

Resilience

Definition:

noun

The capacity to withstand or recover quickly from difficulties.

First used in the 1620s, the word 'resilience' is derived from the Latin *resiliens*, meaning to 'rebound' or 'recoil' back into one's original shape.

"Adversity has the effect of eliciting talents which, in prosperous circumstances, would have lain dormant."

HORACE

Good news! Resilience is not inherited:
it does not appear in your DNA.
You are not born with or without it.
Resilience is instead a set of skills that
can be *learned* to help you survive
through hard times and even to
bounce back better.

"Men's natures are alike; it is their habits that separate them."

CONFUCIUS

"And courage to me meant ploughing through the dull gray mist that comes down on life – not only overriding people and circumstances but overriding the bleakness of living. A sort of insistence on the value of life and the worth of transient things... My courage is faith – faith in the eternal resilience of me – that joy'll come back, and hope and spontaneity. And I feel that till it does I've got to keep my lips shut and my chin high and my eyes wide."

'The Offshore Pirate'
F. SCOTT FITZGERALD

"No pressure, no diamonds."

THOMAS CARLYLE

Resilience reminder

Even if it's not okay, I will be okay.

Monitor your resilience

Machines are constantly monitored for resilience. Picture the dashboard of a car; when some part of the engine requires care and attention, a light will flash – a warning will appear. We too need early warning resilience monitoring.

- Think like an engineer to establish your personal early warning resilience alerts.

- Carefully consider what ought to ring alarm bells – headaches, sleeplessness, shoulder spasms.

- Pay attention to these early warning alerts and take the necessary remedial action.

Q What are the scientific qualities that make a rubber ball bounce back and an iron ball simply thud to the floor?

A The molecules in rubber balls are long and mixed up, which allows them to deform and then reform without breaking, while an iron ball has molecules that are rigid in structure allowing no 'give' or 'bounce' on impact.

To be resilient is to be like the rubber ball: flexible on impact.

"Develop success from failures. Discouragement and failure are two of the surest stepping stones to success."

DALE CARNEGIE

"Nothing in this world can take the place of persistence. Talent will not: nothing is more common than unsuccessful people with talent. Genius will not; unrewarded genius is almost a proverb. Education will not: the world is full of educated derelicts. Persistence and determination alone are omnipotent."

CALVIN COOLIDGE

Five resilience affirmations

1. I am in charge of the problem; the problem is not in charge of me.

2. I can overcome obstacles.

3. I will not let small irritations overwhelm me.

4. I am capable, strong and flexible.

5. I am ready to face challenges big and small.

Resilience is. . .

- Getting up after a knock back.

- Getting up again after the next knock back.

- And again.

- And again.

- And again.

Resilience loves. . . optimism

Nurturing an optimistic outlook helps to create a mindset that sees obstacles and unexpected problems as surmountable rather than instantly problematic and stressful.

Three ways to become more optimistic. . . and eventually resilient

1. Record your achievements daily.

2. Give yourself credit for every small success.

3. Notice and then question pessimistic thoughts.

Dr Samuel Johnson (the 18th-century genius who wrote the first English dictionary) made a series of useful 'instructions' about how to deal with life's 'calamities'.

'Such is the certainty of evil,' he wrote, 'that it is the duty of every man to furnish his mind with those principles that may enable him to act under it with decency and propriety.'

Dr Johnson's instructions greatly emphasized the importance of patience.

" The great remedy which heaven has put in our hands is patience, by which, though we cannot lessen the torments of the body, we can in a great measure preserve the peace of the mind."

DR SAMUEL JOHNSON

Bereavement, separation, illness, medical emergencies, financial issues, natural disasters. . . rare is a life lived that escapes hurt from one or all of the above.

Having resilience does not mean that we don't suffer the pain of such events, but it can help ensure we are not destroyed by them.

Being resilient means being completely at ease with the concept of change – with the understanding that people, circumstances and the daily rhythms of life will always and inevitably change. Being at ease with change is crucial to resilience.

"Remember, no human condition is ever permanent. Then you will not be overjoyed in good fortune nor too scornful in misfortune."

SOCRATES

Viewing yourself as a survivor, not a victim, is a vital part of letting resilience take root.

How to cultivate 'survivor mentality' when in the midst of catastrophe

Remember this acronym: **STOPA**

Sit down.

Take a breath.

Observe your emotional state.

Plan your next move.

Act on that plan.

The life-or-death nature of resilience is captured by the famous ethos of the Navy Seals, the US Navy's primary special operations force.

"I will never quit. I persevere and thrive on adversity. My Nation expects me to be physically harder and mentally stronger than my enemies. If knocked down, I will get back up, every time. I will draw on every remaining ounce of strength to protect my teammates and to accomplish our mission. I am never out of the fight."

While not all of us have the capacity for such extreme resilience, we should consider small ways in which we can practise resilience in our everyday activities.

Like the Navy Seals, resilient people understand that the unexpected is always to be expected.

"It is easy to go down into Hell; night and day the gates of Dark Death stand wide, but to climb back again, to retrace one's steps to the Upper Air – there's the rub, the task."

VIRGIL

Research teaches that how we respond to troubling situations depends significantly on the degree of control we believe we have. If you have a tendency to feel immediately overwhelmed by adversity, get in the habit of deconstructing events to work out what you can control – and what you can't.

The car has locked automatically with the dogs inside.

Remember: don't waste time and emotional energy wildly asking why this happened, whose fault it was or dwelling on what could have prevented the error. Ask yourself: can I control the outcome?

Can you immediately get the dogs out? **No.**

Are they in immediate danger? **No.**

Can you call a neighbour to help? **Yes.**

Can you call the garage? **Yes.**

Can you work out the timings for a rescue? **Yes.**

Deconstructing situational adversity – establishing what you can and can't action – will help create a mindset that is able to positively control difficult situations.

"Don't be afraid to give your best to what seemingly are small jobs. Every time you conquer one it makes you that much stronger. If you do the little jobs well, the big ones will tend to take care of themselves."

DALE CARNEGIE

Resilience requires repetition

By calmly and carefully responding to adversity, you will build up your resilience muscle memory. When a really big disaster strikes, you will slip into resilience mode automatically.

Be resilient. And repeat.

Resilience says. . .

'Yes I can.'

'I will try.'

'Just give me a minute.'

'I will join you.'

'I choose to be here.'

'Can you help me please?'

To fully appreciate what it means to be resilient, reframe your thinking: resilience is not a born quality but a set of habits that you, too, can learn.

Rather than thinking. . .

- She's such a resilient person.

- He's great in a crisis.

- She always knows what to do.

- He's always so calm when he's stressed out.

Think instead...

- She has developed resilient habits.

- He has repeatedly learned how to handle difficult situations.

- She understands what she can and can't control.

- He has developed the ability to remain calm when stressed.

Resilience is all about **GRIT**

Guts.

Resolve.

Industriousness.

Tenacity.

" We first make our habits, then our habits make us."

JOHN DRYDEN

What to do when meeting adversity for the first time

Are you one of those lucky people who have never yet known failure? Did well at school? Had a great prom? Landed the job of your dreams? Life will at some point throw a nasty curve ball. Be prepared.

1. Show gratitude that thus far you have sailed through life unscathed.

2. Remind yourself that everyone fails and experiences negative events.

3. Assess your past successes and work out why they happened.

4. Establish what control you have over your current situation.

5. Plan your way through it.

6. Appreciate that you've taken your first step towards building resilience.

"Concern yourself not with what you tried and failed in, but with what it is still possible for you to do."

POPE JOHN XXII

"If you fell down yesterday, stand up today."

HG WELLS

Unwanted change is deeply distressing. Even desired change can be unsettling. Resilience is fostered in the understanding that everything changes, all the time.

Those who are the most resilient are also those who accept the ebb and flow of life.

" There is nothing in the whole world which abides. All things are in a state of ebb and flow, and every shadow passes away. Even time itself, like a river, is constantly gliding away."

OVID

Five resilience mantras

1. 'I have the courage to carry on.'
2. 'I am bruised but not broken.'
3. 'I will bend but not break.'
4. 'I will inspire others with my strength.'
5. 'I will find another way.'

**Ping. Tweet. Alarm. Snap. Vibrate.
All. The. Time.**

Rare is the person who is not plagued
with constant notifications. We
are expected to reply to messages
IMMEDIATELY. We are in danger of
demanding the same immediate snap
response to all problems.

Let us remind ourselves that not
everything can be resolved instantly.
Resilience asks that we relearn the
art of patience and give ourselves
as much time as is needed to find
solutions.

"Patience is the best remedy for every trouble."

PLAUTUS

How to avoid being brittle

Resilience, which evokes imagery of bouncing back, soft landings and malleable qualities, has its equal and opposite: being brittle. We all know people who are brittle, who over-interpret comments, who snap at the smallest of infractions, who see slights where none are intended. We know it's best to avoid this way of reacting. . . but how?

1. Be sceptical of your own thought patterns. When feeling an emotion ask yourself: am I right to feel this?

2. Give people the benefit of the doubt. You think someone has slighted you – give them another chance. You may be mistaken.

3. Learn to relax and enjoy your own company. Try sitting with your own thoughts for 30 minutes a day.

It may appear unnatural to train ourselves not to feel, not to succumb to the power of emotions, when afflicted by sorrowful or terrifying events. And yet the habit of separating emotion from response, is one that The Stoics explored over 2,000 years ago. At the heart of the Stoic message is the simple idea of not worrying about events beyond our control, summed up by former slave turned philosopher Epictetus who said, 'It is not things that disturb us but rather our opinions of them.'

" Steel your sensibilities, so that life shall hurt you as little as possible."

ZENO OF CITIUM

Three ways Stoic philosophy can foster resilience

1. Practise separating the difficult event from your response to it. Is your reaction making the event worse? How can you respond in a calm and practical way to improve the situation?

2. Practise putting dismal events into perspective. Is the disaster really a calamity or is it just a hiccup? What are you actually able to control?

3. Practise concentrating on the process not the outcome. Understand that there are some things completely outside your control. Concentrate instead on what you can do within the confines of the unknown.

"How does it help... to make troubles heavier by bemoaning them?"

SENECA

We're all guilty of making a rainy day worse by grumbling about the weather. The resilience of the ancient Stoics asks us not to waste emotion on events outside our control. Quit moaning, start planning for indoor fun-times.

Resilience requires an understanding of the concept of *amor fati*.

Latin for 'love of fate', amor fati is a concept whereby everything that happens to you, including sorrow and pain, is beneficial, or at the very least, necessary. Trusting in one's fate during turbulent times can help to bring a sense of perspective, peace and resilience.

" There is a will to live without rejecting anything of life, which is the virtue I honour most in this world."

ALBERT CAMUS

" The longer I live the more I think of the quality of fortitude... men who fall, pick themselves up and stumble on, fall again, and are trying to get back up when they die."

THEODORE ROOSEVELT

"The habit of looking on the bright side of every event is worth more than 1,000 pounds a year."

SAMUEL JOHNSON

A survey into American stress by the Robert Wood Johnson Foundation found that the most popular mood enhancing activities were: time spent outdoors, on a hobby, exercising, enjoying a pet, praying and seeing family and friends.

Work out what makes you feel STRONG

Dedicate an hour to thinking deeply about what you love to do that makes you feel **STRONG, CAPABLE** and **WORTHY**.

Then, diarize time for these activities.

Learn to love manageable stress

Recent research from the Youth Development Initiative at the University of Georgia found that 'low to moderate levels of stress can help individuals develop resilience and reduce the risk of developing mental-health disorders such as depression and antisocial behaviours.'

In much the same way we encourage toddlers to be brave and swing on the monkey bars, teenagers and young adults need to experience low to moderate levels of stress in order to develop cognitive flexibility, resourcefulness and strategies for thriving through adversity.

Understand that resilience doesn't just come after traumatic events. Resilience is a skill that can be mastered before we ever have to use it, with a view to making difficult times more bearable.

3 ways to develop buffer resilience

1. Stay connected: establish and nurture a loving social structure of supportive friends and family.

2. Be self-aware: record every time you respond to a small mishap with proportion and calm competence.

3. Prioritise self-care: create and cultivate a space of complete peace and beauty – your place of safety when times get tough.

The Harvard University Center on the Developing Child uses the image of a see-saw to explain the importance of resilience. On one side are balanced 'protective experiences' and 'coping skills' and on the other is 'adversity'. The key is to tip the seesaw towards positive outcomes even when one side is heavy with negative experiences.

The centre establishes that the *'single most common factor for children who develop resilience is at least one stable and committed relationship with a supportive parent, caregiver or other adult'*.

According to Harvard University's Center on the Developing Child, there are four factors that can support a child in developing a positive attitude when faced with serious adversity.

1. Facilitating supportive adult–child relationships.

2. Building a sense of self-efficacy and perceived control.

3. Providing opportunities to strengthen adaptive skills and self-regulatory capacities.

4. Mobilizing sources of faith, hope and cultural traditions.

Four questions to nourish your most important relationship

1. Who is your most supportive person?

2. Show your most supportive person how much you care for them.

3. Acknowledge and appreciate the protective factor that this relationship offers.

4. Ask yourself how this supportive relationship could be nourished further.

"Nobody trips over mountains. It is the small pebble that causes you to stumble. Pass all the pebbles in your path and you will find you have crossed the mountain."

RALPH WALDO EMERSON

A lesson in resilience from Aesop

An oak and a reed were arguing about their strength. When a strong wind came up, the reed avoided being uprooted by bending and leaning with the gusts of wind. But the oak stood firm and was torn up by the roots.

We are reminded by this wise storyteller that we will all get buffeted by life's hurricanes. What we need is flexibility to bend into stormy weather. By bending and leaning with the wind, the reed survived as the roots remained grounded. Consider your roots as your social support structure and your good habits, enabling you to withstand temporary stormy times.

Ask yourself – *what are my strong foundations that enable me to handle challenging times? What are my good habits that help me to be flexible? Am I able to flex when a new situation arises? What can I do to make sure I don't stiffen and fall?*

Resilience loves. . . self-awareness

Described as the ability to pay attention to your thoughts, emotions, behaviour and psychological reaction to events and people, self-awareness is a crucial tool in resilience development.

Watch yourself

The next time a situation changes
unexpectedly, observe yourself and
monitor your thoughts, emotions and
psychological reactions. For example,
someone accidentally knocks into
you on the tube and you spill coffee
all over yourself. How did you react?
With anger and panic, or with calm
acceptance and planful activity to
rectify the problem? Afterwards,
assess yourself and work out how
you could have handled the situation
to make you more resilient for
future mishaps.

Self-awareness allows for self-correction.

Resilience loves. . . self-regulation

Described as the ability to change one's thoughts, emotions and behaviours in order to achieve a desired outcome, self-regulation is resilience's best friend. A study of Spanish children at risk of social exclusion in *Frontiers of Psychology* confirmed that an ability to self-regulate emotional responses is one of the most protective factors in fostering resilience.

Step outside the catastrophe

During an emotional event, if possible, take time to step outside and look in as if you were a caring outsider.

How would you like the caring person to respond?

How would they react positively?

How would they work to resolve, rather than escalate, things?

Now return yourself to the situation and regulate your behaviour to be purposeful and positive. In doing so, you will demonstrate to yourself that you are able not only to take useful control over a situation, but also over yourself.

Resilience understands the importance of 'benefit finding' – that is, seeing the potential for positive growth in adversity.

Take the 'silver linings' challenge

Challenge yourself to find a 'benefit'
for every negative that crops up,
big or small. If the disaster is too
catastrophic to 'find the good',
at least ask yourself, what am
I learning from this?

"Behind the cloud the sun is still shining."

ABRAHAM LINCOLN

"Difficulties are meant to rouse, not discourage. The human spirit is to grow strong by conflict."

WILLIAM ELLERY CHANNING

It helps to recognize that resilience isn't only helpful during life-altering calamities, but also during the small stresses of daily life. A passive-aggressive conversation with a romantic partner or an unexpected call with an irate colleague can all activate the stress response, thus demanding resilience.

Time yourself returning to calm

Next time a small stress arrives – let's say you have to take a detour on your way to work – time yourself. Record how long it takes to shut off the stress response and return to baseline tranquillity. Are you still fuming about the detour at coffee time, lunchtime, dinnertime? Aim to reduce the time spent in a state of stress.

Journal moments of gratitude

Record every time you are grateful for showing resilience. No matter how small the stress that was overcome, show gratitude for your ability to deploy a resilient response.

Journal your way to resilience with affirmations

Focus on aspects of your character, values and habits that support resilience. Use as your prompts:

I am not easily thrown off course.
I am calm under pressure.
I reset my sails quickly when needed.

Journal honestly

Telling yourself honest truths about how your deepest fears did not come to pass will help develop resilience. Use as your prompts:

This is an example of my fear being proved wrong...
I understand I am unrealistic to fear this because...
Here are three examples to remind me that I can cope with tricky times...

Journal your responses

Analyzing how you responded to a stressful situation during the day can assist in clarifying what more you need to do to encourage resilience. Use as your prompts:

I am pleased / disappointed with how I responded to. . .
Next time a similar situation arises I will. . .
In order to make a swifter return to equilibrium after stress I will focus on. . .

Journal for a confidence boost

Having a firm sense of your own abilities to regulate emotions and solve problems will help reinforce a resilience mindset.

I am capable of seeing the positive in the negative.
I am competent in a crisis.
I keep a sense of perspective in difficult times.

(Remember the golden rule for journalling: always buy the most beautiful notebook you can afford so it becomes a luxurious pleasure to fill its pages.)

Poetry for resilience

Goblin Market is a tantalizing poem by Victorian poet Christina Rossetti. She tells of two sisters, Lizzie and Laura, who are tempted by the addictive fruits of the Goblin Market. Laura begins to waste away in her pursuit of the Goblin fruit but Lizzie is able to resist. Eventually Lizzie finds a way to rescue her sister from the clutches of the goblins and their fruit. This heart-wrenching poem is a dramatic reminder that resilience is not just useful for selfish reasons, but necessary at times to help our nearest and dearest.

"For there is no friend like a sister
In calm or stormy weather;
To cheer one on the tedious way,
To fetch one if one goes astray,
To lift one if one totters down,
To strengthen whilst one stands."

CHRISTINA ROSSETTI

For times when we feel that life
is giving us a savage battering,
turn to the poem Good Timber by
Douglas Malloch, American poet and
lumberman. He fully recognised that
to grow true and strong, a certain
amount of hardship was necessary. . .
and that we can withstand it.

"The tree that never had to fight
For sun and sky and air and light,
But stood out in the open plain
And always got its share of rain,
Never became a forest king
But lived and died a scrubby thing.

The man who never had to toil
To gain and farm his patch of soil,
Who never had to win his share
Of sun and sky and light and air,
Never became a manly man
But lived and died as he began.

Good timber does not grow with ease,
The stronger wind, the stronger trees,
The further sky, the greater length,
The more the storm, the more the strength.
By sun and cold, by rain and snow,
In trees and men, good timbers grow.

Where thickest lies the forest growth
We find the patriarchs of both.
And they hold counsel with the stars
Whose broken branches show the scars
Of many winds and much of strife.
This is the common law of life."

DOUGLAS MALLOCH

What is nature if not resilient to the icy grip of winter? When the land appears barren, life huddles in the cold earth waiting to emerge. Spring launches itself from the dreary cold in a burst of colour, birdsong and gentle sunshine. Spring is our annual reminder that no matter how unpromising and frigid everything seems, better times *will come*.

"Winter always turns into spring. Never, from ancient times on, has anyone heard or seen of winter turning back to autumn."

NICHIREN

This gentle poem by A.E. Housman, 'Lovliest of trees, the cherry now', describes a 20-year-old realizing he may have only another 50 years to enjoy spring's unfurling beauty. He wistfully captures the recognition that life is brief. An appreciation of this fact within the context of spring's fleeting prettiness helps us to understand that resilience is deeply embedded into all of nature.

"Loveliest of trees, the cherry now
Is hung with bloom along the bough,
And stands about the woodland ride
Wearing white for Eastertide.

Now, of my threescore years and ten,
Twenty will not come again,
And take from seventy springs a score,
It only leaves me fifty more.

And since to look at things in bloom
Fifty springs are little room,
About the woodlands I will go
To see the cherry hung with snow."

A.E. HOUSMAN

The joy of being resilient is that once the hard times have passed and you are still standing, everyday beauty becomes all the more exquisite.

"For winter's rains and ruins are over,
And all the season of snows and sins;
The days dividing lover and lover,
The light that loses, the night that wins;
And time remembered is grief forgotten,
And frosts are slain and flowers begotten,
And in green underwood and cover
Blossom by blossom the spring begins."

ALGERNON CHARLES SWINBURNE

"I am not afraid of storms for I am learning how to sail my ship."

LOUISA MAY ALCOTT

"If we had not winter, the spring would not be so pleasant; if we did not sometimes taste of adversity, prosperity would not be so welcome."

ANNE BRADSTREET

Visualize resilience as building blocks

Let's say you've had a terrible experience ordering food in a restaurant. You messed up the order, everyone got the wrong dishes, the waitress was embarrassed and the evening was ruined. See this incident as: one building block.

You are faced with two options now:

1. Never order food in a restaurant again.

2. Have another go. And another, and another.

View each effort – each time you try again – as its own building block. Every time you decide to have another go, you place one building block on top of the previous. Soon, you will have built a tower of resilience that dwarfs the tiny disaster you created earlier.

The resilient mental toolkit

- Optimism
- Creative thinking
- Problem solving
- Serenity under pressure
- Self-control
- Self-belief
- Patience

Something's gone wrong... Who do you want to be?

The calmest person in the room or the one shouting **PANIC**?

Who do you think is most resilient?

Without sufficient sleep, resilience eludes us all; we are instead plagued with brain fog, snappy tempers and physical exhaustion. This makes us brittle and less likely to flex in and out of setbacks.

Three ways to prioritize sleep for resilience

1. Set a regular bedtime (adults need between 7-9 hours' sleep a night).

2. Keep screens out of bedrooms.

3. Relax before you attempt to go to sleep, either with a warm bath, reading in bed or evening meditation.

Resilience is a skill that is best practised when life is humming along happily. It's almost too late to begin attempting resilience in times of catastrophe. In times of flourishing happiness, develop resilient routines.

1. Assess your daily routines – are there areas that could be streamlined to work better for you?

2. Assess your values – are you prioritizing the values that are most important to you?

3. Assess your problems / fears – are you setting goals in order to productively work through your problems?

Five thought disciplines that foster resilience

1. Gratitude: the art of being grateful for outcomes, no matter how disappointing, helps us to move on after trying times.

2. Forgiveness: hanging on to negative encounters or criticisms can slow the return to equilibrium. Rather than ruminating or plotting revenge, embrace forgiveness.

3. The ability to pause: just spending a few seconds breathing deeply can be enough to moderate your response to an upset.

4. Bravery to face your fears: expose yourself to situations that are safe but you fear are not, in order to reduce your anxiety response.

5. The ability to seek the good: develop the habit of looking squarely at negative events to find the good hidden within.

Six habits that cultivate resilience

We've all been there, when a tiny incident is enough to send us to the floor in a puddle of tears. At that moment our burdens are too great for us to withstand even the smallest of hiccups, and being resilient feels impossible. Yet, there are habits we can cultivate to protect ourselves even when we are fully laden with the pressures of life. If we manage to live a happy, healthy, orderly life, no matter how many problems batter us at once, we will be better able to remain upright.

1. Prioritize your loved ones: your social support network is what will get you through difficult times, actively love and support your nearest and dearest.

2. Practise good sleep hygiene: regular bedtimes, no screens, and attempt 7–9 hours a night.

3. Eat healthily: enjoy a nutritious diet – the sort of food your grandparents would recognize.

4. Stay fit: work a fitness regime into your daily life, a brisk walk, a short workout, a stint of yoga – whatever makes you move around happily.

5. Organize the small stuff: keep that drawer full of spare batteries, light bulbs, thank you cards, Sellotape, extra chargers, plasters, antihistamines, nail scissors and other such things well-stocked and orderly.

6. Regularly audit finances: assess your income, accounts and investments regularly in order to maintain mastery over this crucial aspect of life.

Remember what your grandmother used to say: *"Worse things happen at sea."*

This rather opaque saying is there to offer solidarity at times of hardship with others who are suffering. Casting our minds away from our present trouble to consider the plight of others also reassures us that challenges are surmountable. Eventually the storm will pass.

Resilience requires you to put your energy in the right place.

Energy, like time, is not an infinite resource. In the heat of the moment, be mindful where you put your energy. Are you huffing and puffing about why everything has gone wrong, or quietly contemplating a solution? After the initial emergency has passed, do you continue to rage about the incident or do you competently prepare strategies to stop similar events happening again?

Treat your own energy like gold and distribute it wisely.

" Energy and persistence conquer all things."

BENJAMIN FRANKLIN

Delve into your family history for stories of resilience

It is always worth remembering that being alive today requires having ancestors who survived **EVERYTHING** that 300,000 years of human history had to throw at them: wars, plague, natural disasters, the whole ugly gamut. Within your **DNA** lies the untold stories of ancestors who triumphed over sabre toothed tigers, famines, medieval battlefields, 1970s Angel Delight... to pass on their genes to now living descendants.

While it's impossible to unearth all ancestral tales of resilience, it is always deeply nourishing to seek inspiration from the oldest members of your family tree.

Six questions to ask family members about ancestral resilience

1. What challenges have you overcome?

2. How did you keep going through difficult times?

3. What stories can you remember your parents and grandparents telling you about tough times?

4. Who in our family tree do you most admire and why?

5. What do you believe is our special family strength?

6. What is your one piece of advice for coping and continuing on?

" The hero draws inspiration from the virtue of his ancestors."

JOHANN GOETHE

Fatalism and realism come in handy when resilience is required. Optimism is desirable for positive living, but to foster conditions that forge resilience for life's inevitable challenges, you must keep in touch with the grim reality that all life ends in death. There will be sorrow and pain along the way.

If you expect winter to be cold, you will prepare for the big freeze and settle in and wait for spring to come. If you're still swanning around in flips flops and have forgotten to order the logs, the icy grip of winter will be painful to bear. Be realistic about what life will throw at you and prepare your defences.

"Everything passes away – suffering, pain, blood, hunger, pestilence. The sword will pass away too, but the stars will remain when the shadows of our presence and our deeds have vanished from the Earth. There is no man who does not know that. Why, then, will we not turn our eyes toward the stars? Why?"

MIKHAIL BULGAKOV

Six resilience mantras

1. 'I will find the positives in the pain.'

2. 'What doesn't defeat me fortifies me.'

3. 'I am resourceful. I am optimistic. I am successful.'

4. 'I am flexible and will bend when required.'

5. 'With courage I will continue.'

6. 'I am brave. I am strong. I will be okay.'

Resilience role model Gene 'Work the Problem' Kranz

Imagine you're the lead flight director of a mission to the moon, your team of astronauts are 200,000 miles away from earth and **BOOM!** There's an explosion: *'Houston, we have a problem.'* Step forward Gene Kranz, lead flight director of NASA flight Apollo 13. Famously portrayed by Ed Harris in the blockbuster *Apollo 13*, Gene Krantz came to epitomize the calm, level-headed, solution-based leader that saw the safe return of the astronauts to earth.

Decreasing oxygen levels, lack of
power, panic, loss of water and total
dread were problems that gripped
the NASA team. In the early hours
of the accident, Gene Krantz's
approach to the unfolding potential
catastrophe was to 'Work the problem.'
He apparently chanted 'Work the
problem', after every obstacle, saying,
'Don't make it worse by guessing.'

The three astronauts transferred
from the Command Module to Lunar
Module Aquarius and, five days
after the explosion, safely splashed
back down to Earth. Gene Kranz
and the rest of the NASA team had
successfully 'worked the problem'.

How to 'work the problem', NASA style

1. Establish *exactly* what the problem is.

2. Break it into small parts.

3. Work *each* problem.

In 2022, *The Times* ran an Education Commission with 12 ideas to improve British education. As part of their research, journalists interviewed adventurer Bear Grylls, who was adamant that resilience should be taught in schools. He said, 'You've got to honour resilience. You've got to teach resilience. You've got to praise it. You've got to give focus to it.'

Bear Grylls has set up a foundation that teaches schoolchildren that 'greatness isn't born, it is learned.'

Resilience role model Arthur Ashkin

If anyone can teach you that it is never too later to keep going, it's Arthur Ashkin, who won the Nobel Prize for Physics at the age of 96. Born in Brooklyn in 1922 to a Jewish–Ukrainian family, Arthur Ashkin dedicated his whole life to science, receiving his PhD from Cornell in 1952. He advanced the fields of photorefraction, second harmonic generation and non-linear optics in fibres. He finally won the Nobel Prize for inventing 'optical tweezers', a vital tool in modern day nanotechnology and biological systems which 'catches' bacteria and other tiny particles with light. He initially faced widespread scepticism but his perseverance epitomizes the relentless application of an inquiring mind.

Resilience role model Antonie van Leeuwenhoek

It's the 17th century in the Dutch Republic and a young man has created his own single-lensed microscope. He scoops up a bit of pond water and watches, astonished, as tiny 'animalcules' swarm about. He was one of the first men on earth to 'see' microscopic life forms. Antonie van Leeuwenhoek writes excitedly to The Royal Society in London with details of his discovery and is met with a wall of establishment silence. No-one is interested in the amateur tinkering of this boorish Dutchman. Yet Antonie van Leeuwenhoek does not give up. He continues battering the scientific community with letters: over 500 in all, including 190 to the Royal Society. After many years of being written off as a Lowland amateur, Antonie van Leeuwenhoek is eventually elected to the Royal Society in 1680. He is now known as the father of microbiology and is recognized as one of the greatest Dutchmen of all time.

Resilience role model Gertrude 'Queen of the Waves' Ederle

Gertrude Ederle was taught to swim in the Shrewsbury River in New Jersey by her father, who tied a rope around her waist, before suffering a bout of the measles that damaged her ears. She was warned that swimming would make her hearing loss worse. Nevertheless, in 1920, at the age of 15, she became the first woman to swim the length of New York Bay. By 1929 she had smashed 29 women's front crawl records. Her first attempt

at swimming the English Channel
in 1925 was disqualified, but she
eventually succeeded in 1926. Her
swim lasted 14 hours and 39 minutes,
beating the men's record by two hours.
Sadly, the swimming *did* further
damage her hearing, but she dedicated
the latter part of her life to teaching
deaf children to swim. She died in
2003 at the age of 98.

Resilience role model Sheryl Sandberg

Famous for inspiring women to 'lean in' to their careers, the former chief operating officer of META (Facebook), Sheryl Sandberg seemed to embody the woman who combined a happy family life with a flourishing career. In a reminder that tragedy comes to the most successful and fortunate of people, her husband died unexpectedly in 2015. Sheryl Sandberg's world capsized. So how does the titan of Silicon Valley work

through this emotional tragedy?
She reaches out to her support
structure and researches the problem.
Sheryl Sandberg reached out to a
psychologist friend of hers, whose
day job consisted of helping people
to find meaning in their lives. The
psychologist directed her to ideas of
resilience, recommending she research
how others navigate grief and similar
challenges. If Sheryl Sandberg is able
to ask for help and seek inspiration
from others, so can we.

Be resilient the Sheryl Sandberg way. If disaster strikes:

1. Seek solace within your family.

2. Reach out to experts for support.

3. Read deeply into the problem to equip yourself with knowledge for the way forward.

"It is really wonderful how much resilience there is in human nature. Let any obstructing cause, no matter what, be removed in any way – even by death – and we fly back to first principles of hope and enjoyment."

BRAM STOKER

Praise resilience where you find it

Make a conscious effort to elevate and laud resilience when you see it in others. Whenever your parent, colleague or flatmate demonstrates resilience, celebrate with them. A gentle word of acknowledgment showing respect for their courage and persistence can be enough to further embed the practice in both them and yourself.

"What's the point?" "We're all going to die." "It's not worth it."

Nihilism. Existential angst. Despair. These feelings afflict everyone at some point. It is at such times of bottomless despair that resilience is most required. How then are we to reach for hope when everything seems pointless?

Poet and visionary William Blake has the answer: with love, as he writes in *Songs of Experience* (1794).

" Love seeketh not itself to please,
Nor for itself hath any care,
But for another gives its ease,
And builds a Heaven in Hell's despair."

WILLIAM BLAKE

When wretched with despair, remember the words of William Blake and return to love

Ask yourself:

- Who loves you?

- Who do you love?

- What do you love?

- How can you show love?

- What acts of love can you attempt?

Root yourself in love and begin
to rebuild.

Remember that to an ant, a molehill is a mountain and to a pilot, a mountain is a molehill. Your response to an obstacle very much depends on your perspective. Cultivate your ability to focus and refocus to keep obstacles in appropriate perspective.

"A weak mind is like a microscope which magnifies trifling things, but cannot receive great ones."

LORD CHESTERFIELD

Be mindful of the dangers of 'safetyism'

There has been recent pushback against the trend of safetyism within the psychotherapy community. Public intellectuals including Jonathan Haidt and Matthew B. Crawford have warned that attempting to protect children and teenagers from all emotional and physical harm actually prevents them from developing resilience.

By shielding people from harm, a destructive feedback loop is created whereby children become more fragile and thus require more protection. Instead, we need to be honest with each other about the importance of experiencing a certain amount of physical stress and emotional discomfort in order to develop capable coping mechanisms.

Go on a news fast

Choose a day or two a week where you completely avoid engaging with the day's news. Free yourself from the stress and worry of local and world news. Return to the fray the following day with a calmer mind.

" *There will always be rocks in the road ahead of us. They will be stumbling blocks or stepping stones; it all depends on how you use them.* "

NIETZSCHE

" Colin flushed triumphantly. He had made himself believe that he was going to get well, which was really more than half the battle, if he had been aware of it."

FRANCES HODGSON BURNETT

"As Clara had no chair to go in and yet wanted so much to see the flowers, she made the effort to walk, and every day since she has been walking better and better, and if she remains up here she will in time be able to go up the mountain every day, much oftener than she would have done in her chair."

JOHANNA SPYRI

For billions of people around the globe, a base note of faith is the tune that helps them sing the song of resilience. Explore different faith traditions, visit local faith centres and be inspired by those for whom faith sustained them during challenging periods. And let's be honest here, when we require resilience, it is immensely encouraging to feel the head wind of an all-powerful deity behind us, guiding us onward.

Resilient people...

- Anticipate rejection and setbacks.

- Don't expect everything to
  be perfect.

- Do not dwell on why something
  went wrong but on how to improve
  the situation.

Resilience in extremis

On the wild, windswept, 19th-century Yorkshire moors lived the Brontë family. The six children created novels, poetry and characters that still move our hearts centuries later: Heathcliff and Cathy haunting Wuthering Heights; Jane Eyre, Mr Rochester and the incarcerated Mrs Rochester of Thornfield Hall. But the astonishing creative richness of the six Brontë children, Maria, Elizabeth, Charlotte, Branwell, Emily and Anne was not matched with physical robustness.

Charlotte Brontë watched all of her
five siblings die. She lived another
six years before her own death
during pregnancy. In one of her most
poignant letters, Charlotte Brontë
describes how her faith in God,
and the support of loving friends,
sustained her during a year of
three deaths.

" *There must be heaven or we must despair, for life seems bitter, brief – blank...A year ago – had a prophet warned me how I should stand in June 1849 – how stripped and bereaved – had he foretold the autumn – the winter, the spring of sickness and suffering to be gone through – I should have thought – this can never be endured. It is over. Branwell – Emily – Anne are gone like dreams – gone as Maria and Elizabeth went twenty years ago. One by one I have watched them fall asleep on my arm – and closed their glazed eyes – I have seen them buried one by one – and – thus far – God has upheld me. From my heart I thank him.*

I thank too the friends whose sympathy has given me inexpressible comfort and strength."

CHARLOTTE BRONTË

" *The soul is dyed the colour of its thoughts. Think only on those things that are in line with your principles and can bear the light of day. The content of your character is your choice. Day by day, what you choose, what you think, and what you do is who you become. Your integrity is your destiny… it is the light that guides your way.*"

HERACLITUS

" *Out of suffering comes the serious mind; out of salvation, the grateful heart; out of endurance, fortitude; out of deliverance faith. Patient endurance attends to all things.* "

ST TERESA OF AVILA

After the death of the last of her five siblings in 1849, Charlotte Brontë, author of *Jane Eyre*, is faced with the dismal prospect of returning to their family home of Haworth Parsonage to see her father. In her letters, she describes how she the bitter grief envelop her, until she begins writing in an effort to relieve her deep sorrow. She eventually published her most complex and most autobiographical novel, *Villette*, in 1853.

In this extreme example of fortitude and resilience, Charlotte Brontë reminds us that just as others have persevered through suffering, so too can we.

"*All this bitterness must be tasted – perhaps the palate will grow used to the draught in time and find its flavour less acrid – this pain must be undergone – its poignancy I trust – will be blunted one day... I knew it would be better to face the desolation at once – later or sooner the sharp pang must be experienced.*

Labour must be the cure, not sympathy – Labour is the only radical cure for rooted sorrow – the society of a calm, serenely cheerful companion... soothes pain like a soft opiate – but

I find it does not probe or heal the wound – sharper more severe means are necessary to make a remedy. Total change might do much – where that cannot be obtained – work is the best substitute."

CHARLOTTE BRONTË

A note from the author

In May 2022, my 13-year-old niece Annabel Remmer had her left leg amputated following a diagnosis of osteosarcoma and a gruelling course of chemotherapy. Since then, she has had a prosthetic leg fitted, learned to ski again, played football in the UEFA amputee football programme, been signed as a model with Zebedee talent, been voted Head Girl of her comprehensive in Staffordshire,

England and performed with Sam Ryder at the Eurovision Song Contest Final in 2023. Annabel is the High Princess of Resilience. Her motto is: 'I am not happened to me. I am what I choose to become.' You can follow her uplifting journey of resilience and joy at www.annabelkiki.com.

PEOPLE QUOTED

Abraham Lincoln, 1809–1865, 16th President of the United States

A.E. Housman, 1859–1936, English poet

Alexander Dumas, 1802–1870, French writer

Alexander Pushkin, 1799–1837, Russian poet

Algernon Charles Swinburne, 1837–1909, English poet and playwright

Anne Bradstreet, 1612–1672, American poet

Benjamin Franklin, 1706–1790, American polymath and founding father

Bram Stoker, 1847–1912, Irish author

Calvin Coolidge, 1872–1933, 30th President of the United States

Charlotte Brontë, 1816–1855, English novelist

Christina Rossetti, 1830–1894, English poet

Confucius, 551–479 BCE, Chinese philosopher

Dale Carnegie, 1888–1955, American writer and lecturer

Douglas Malloch, 1877–1938, American poet and author

Dr Samuel Johnson, 1709–1784, English writer and lexicographer

F. Scott Fitzgerald, 1896–1940, American author

Friedrich Nietzsche, 1844–1900, German philosopher

Frances Hodgson Burnett, 1849–1924, English author

Heraclitus, c.540–470 BCE, Greek philosopher

HG Wells, 1866–1946, English writer

Johann Wolfgang von Goethe, 1749–1832, German writer

Johanna Spyri, 1827–1901, Swiss author

John Dryden, 1631–1700, English poet
and playwright

Lord Chesterfield, 1694–1773, English statesman
and writer

Louisa May Alcott, 1832–1888, American author

Mahatma Gandhi, 1869–1948, Indian lawyer, anti-
colonial nationalist and civil rights activist

Mikhail Bulgakov, 1891–1940, Russian novelist
and playwright

Mirabai, 1498–1547, Indian mystic poet

Nichiren, 1222–1282, Japanese Buddhist monk

Ovid, 43 BCE–17 AD, Roman poet

Plautus, 254–184 BCE, Roman playwright

Pope John XXII, 1215–1334, Pope of the Catholic
Church

Ralph Waldo Emerson, 1803–1882, American poet, essayist and philosopher

Seneca, 4 BCE–65 AD, Roman Stoic philosopher

Socrates, 469–399 BCE, Greek philosopher

St. Teresa of Avila, 1515–1582, Spanish mystic and saint

Theodore Roosevelt, 1858–1919, 26th President of the United States

Thomas Carlyle, 1795–1881, Scottish historian, essayist and literary critic

Virgil, 70–19 BCE, Roman epic poet

William Ellery Channing, 1780–1842, American Unitarian minister and philosopher

Zeno of Citium, 334–262 BCE, Greek philosopher

USEFUL WEBSITES

berkeleywellbeing.com

manifestationbabe.com

mindbodygreen.com

oprahdaily.com

thelawofattraction.com

roxienafousi.com

USEFUL BOOKS

The Resilience Factor: Seven Keys to Finding Your Inner Strength and Overcoming Life's Hurdles by Rick Hanson

Resilience: The Science of Mastering Life's Greatest Challenges by Steven Pressfield

The Upside of Stress: Why the Most Resilient People Thrive Under Pressure by Kelly McGonigal

Man's Search for Meaning by Viktor E. Frankl

Daring Greatly: How the Courage to Be Vulnerable Transforms the Way We Live, Love, Parent, and Lead by Brené Brown

The Power of Vulnerability: Teachings on Authenticity, Connection, and Courage by Brené Brown

The Untethered Soul: The Journey Beyond Yourself by Michael A Singer

USEFUL RESILIENCE COURSE

The Penn Resilience Program (PRP) and PERMA™ Workshops are evidence-based training programs that have been demonstrated to build resilience, well-being, and optimism.
https://ppc.sas.upenn.edu/services/penn-resilience-training

ARTICLES REFERRED TO

'Is perceived stress linked to enhanced cognitive functioning and reduced risk for psychopathology? Testing the hormesis hypothesis', Oshri. A, et al., *Psychiatry Research* 2022.

'Relationship between Resilience and Self-regulation: A Study of Spanish Youth at Risk of Social Exclusion.', Artuch-Garde. R, et al., *Front Psychol* 8(612), 2017.
doi: 10.3389/fpsyg.2017.00612.

'Trigger Warnings Are Trivially Helpful at Reducing Negative Affect, Intrusive Thoughts, and Avoidance', Sanson. M., et al., *Clinical Psychological Science* 7(4), 778–793, 2019.

Managing Director Sarah Lavelle
Assistant Editor Sofie Shearman
Words Joanna Gray
Series Designer Emily Lapworth
Designer Katy Everett
Head of Production Stephen Lang
Production Controller Martina Georgieva

Published in 2023 by Quadrille,
an imprint of Hardie Grant
Publishing

Quadrille
52–54 Southwark Street
London SE1 1UN
quadrille.com

Compilation, design, layout and text
© 2023 Quadrille

The publisher has made every
effort to trace the copyright
holders. We apologize in advance
for any unintentional omissions
and would be pleased to insert the
appropriate acknowledgement in
any subsequent edition.

Cataloguing in Publication Data:
a catalogue record for this book is
available from the British Library.

ISBN 978 1 83783 052 7

Printed in China

MIX
Paper | Supporting
responsible forestry
FSC® C020056